Xbox Hip Hop And Dreadlocks

"Reconnecting the Generations"

By: Randolph B. Lewis

FIRST EDITION 2011

Xbox, HipHop and Dreadlocks
"Reconnecting the Generations"

COPYRIGHT © 2011 by Randolph B. Lewis

All rights reserved. No part of this publication may be reproduced, stored in a retrieval system, or transmitted in any form or by any means, electronic, mechanical, photocopying, recording or otherwise, without the prior written permission of the publisher.

ISBN 978-0-615-45995-0

Published by Lewis Maxwell Training

Design and Layout by Janine Lewis

Printed in the United States of America

Table of Contents

Acknowledgements	*Page 5*
Forward	*Page 7*
Introduction	*Page 10*
Understanding Youth	*Page 14*
Three "R"s of Communication	*Page 16*
The Time Machine	*Page 20*
Driving Forces	*Page 22*
Microwave vs. Lay-A-Way	*Page 41*
Big Question	*Page 45*
Strategies	*Page 47*
Re-Creation	*Page 52*
Closing	*Page 55*
About the Author	*Page 57*
Memories	*Page 63*
References	*Page 67*

This book is dedicated to the memory of my grandmother Caretha Kitchen, father Willie "Bones" Lewis, mother Jean A. Lewis, my two favorite aunts Altamease Banks and Gladys Bethea. Thank you for all the love, guidance and support you have given to me throughout life. Thanks for standing in the gap and helping to mold me.

I love you all!!!

Acknowledgements

No undertaking of this magnitude is possible without the support and affirmation of many special people. I wish to thank the following persons who delicately balanced the criticism and encouragement which helped to enhance the overall quality of this book. I am grateful to my NABCJ friends Lola Wrenn, Candace Thomas and Angela Tomlinson who initially encouraged me to write this book. I am grateful to Dr. Yvonne Williams and Diane Marcou who read my manuscript and gave me friendly criticism.

I am indebted to my children Christopher, Britteny, Brandon and Micah for their contributions to this book and the sacrifice each made to assist with this project.

I am grateful for the love, prayers and assistance of my wife, Janine and all the sacrifices she made to support me during this journey. Your love and understanding mean the world to me.

A special thank and shout out to my friends, Dr. Randy B. Nelson and Karen Pierce. I want to personally thank all my siblings especially my brothers

Rev. G. Vincent Lewis and Dr. Lafayette Maxwell for believing in me and encouraging me from the beginning. To my mentor, Bishop Rudolph W. McKissick, Sr., thank you for leading by example. Your lessons on the importance of putting God first, ceaseless prayer and the value of education have been invaluable during life's good times and challenges.

No dream is possible without Faith. I thank God for blessing me with the gifts of compassion and expression. These gifts have allowed me to uplift youth and attempt to reconnect the generations.

There have been many people in my life that have helped me along the way. I can't begin to thank them all, so to each of you collectively, Thank you!

Forward:

Train up a child in the way he should go:
And when he is old, he will not depart from it.
Proverbs 22:6

I am both BLESSED and honored to write the forward to a book that attempts to approach the disconnect between adults and today's youth. 2008 was a challenging year for our family. We endured many heart aches, and came to terms with a number of grave losses. Over the course of our marriage Randy and I have had many debates about the differences between the experiences of today's youth, and our individual adolescent and young adulthood experiences. Xbox, Hip-Hop and Dreadlocks is the summation of our research which stemmed from those debates and discussions. Our 1970's Southern traditional childhood experiences differed greatly. I enjoyed the benefits of having middle class parents, and he grew up poor. When we met and married we became a blended family, and the entire household quickly realized that he and I had differing parenting philosophies. We have reared four children to young adulthood. It has not been easy, but it has been insightful. Many believe that a veil exists between the youth of today and their adult caregivers. It is our belief that if you are willing to approach the veil and peer between the weave you will be amazed. From afar the picture behind the veil appears foreign, but upon closer inspection it looks very much the same as our youthful days. To touch the life of a child is rewarding in many respects. Randy has touched the lives of many young people in the 1970's as "Fluffy Puppy" teaching spiritual lessons to toddlers many seasons past, as a father, youth mentor and teacher today. It is a calling that he has embraced and labors at ceaselessly. His proactive approach to communicating and interacting with youth yields great dividends. He has enjoyed a number of graduations that other's thought not possible. He has touched the lives of many, who have paid it forward and touched the lives of others. It is exponential in scope. The task requires time and sacrifice for which he gives freely. To look into his childhood, this humble, funny man was a middle child who was quick to "crack" jokes, and slow to self motivate. His most memorable life lessons were received while spending time with his maternal grandmother. He has been blessed beyond measure. It is our belief that to whom much is given much is required. Randy is a bridge builder. He builds the bridge not for his own use, but for those who will follow.

Janine Lewis

Xbox, Hip Hop and Dreadlocks

Introduction

Drastic times have demanded drastic measures throughout American History. Families have changed! Teenagers today *appear* to be very different from teenagers of yesterday. Are they really that different? The workshop, *"Xbox, Hip Hop and Dreadlocks"*, explored the three driving forces that influence behavior in youth: Music, Media, and Peers.

In X-Box, Hip Hop and Dreadlocks strategies geared toward improving our ability to approach, communicate, and interact on a positive level with youth are introduced, developed, and analyzed. Each segment identifies what today's youth "really want". The primary factors that drive the decision making process of youth and their views of success are explored. Can they be motivated? If so what prerequisites are needed to relate to this group of youth who live in a digital age and experience life on a global scale?

In the segment, "Time Machine" an interactive exercise is introduced that requires participants to go back in time to their teen age years in the 60's, 70's or 80's. As a group the importance of self expression is explored. How does it sound and appear in an age that allows freedom of expression when the parameters restricting expression can border profanity and pornographic images?

The Afro, Hip Huggers, Atari games, and Marvin Gaye's song "What's Going On" voiced the uniqueness of the 60's, 70's or 80's. Sagging jeans, Dread Locks, Xbox games and Tupac's "Keep Your Head Up" gives a glimpse of the uniqueness of today's youth. Youth of Today want the same things as the Youth of Yesterday:

- **They want to be safe**
- **They want to feel cared for**

- They want to be valued
- They want to be useful
- They want to have a sense of Belonging
- They want to be Successful

The purpose of the workshop is to engage the participants in exercises forcing them to look at the trends of today from a different point of view. The sensationalism is peeled away, and key issues facing today's youth are discussed. An understanding of the similarities of youth today and the youth of yesteryear is the objective of the workshop. At the conclusion of this workshop attendees will have insight into the pressures and challenges facing the youth of today. Participants are left with perplexing thoughts to ponder and a different view of the factors that shape modern culture. In a global world where music, media and peers have more clout than a parent's lamented words of wisdom - the ability to connect and communicate is the key.

Throughout the presentation acknowledgement that today's youth are smarter, less forgiving and more confrontational is recognized, yet their primary needs are universal needs that have spanned generations. When adults realize this, the task of guiding the future leaders of tomorrow becomes very manageable.

UNDERSTANDING YOUTH

When an in depth look at the youth of today is taken one will find that they possess the same needs, ask the same questions, and seek the same reassurances as their parents did when they were young. Every generation vows they are smarter than their parents, and will not make the same mistakes.

Academic aptitudes of today have surpassed the academic aptitudes of the past, and while that fact must be recognized - a mechanism to impart wisdom must be devised. With this thought in mind it is important to understand what young people want, and find ways to communicate with them to bring about mutual understanding.

In my twenty-five plus years of working with youth, in both a personal and professional capacity, I have come across the very same wants expressed or implied by young people. It has become very apparent to me that all youth seek and want the following six (6) things:

- **They want to be safe**- Everyone has a "basic" need for safety and want to feel protected in their home, school, community, work place, etc.

- **They want to feel cared for-** To know that someone loves them based on their actions and not just words alone. Men sometimes have a hard time expressing this message to boys mainly because they were taught not to express their emotions, and especially not to someone of the same gender.

- **They want to be valued-** Adults should not make kids feel worthless by talking down to them. Self worth can be fostered in young people early through constant encouragement.

- **They want to be useful-** Adults should assign chores or other tasks and make sure the young people complete those given assignments regardless of how long it takes. Adults should be careful not to take over the assignments due to impatience. Taking over the assignment sends a message of uselessness, and that it's okay not to complete something that they start.

- **They want to have a sense of Belonging-** Everyone values friendships and group associations. They want to be a part of the "in" crowd.

- **They want to be Successful-** They want to be able live the life of "success" that they see on TV, Movies, etc....Nice car, House, Clothes, Etc.

When an honest assessment is taken, you will find that they want the same things that all people at their age wanted and in some case still want as an adult!!

The Three R's of Communications

In a global world where music, media and peers have more clout than a parent's lamented words of wisdom - the ability to connect and communicate is the key. Adults, both past and present, have struggled with trying to bridge the "communication gap" as it relates to connecting with young adults. Most of this failure to connect can be found primary in the way most adults approach the interaction.

Parents/Adults tend to talk at or down to youth as a way of establishing their parental/adult authority. This type of communication immediately places the youth on the defense causing them to shutdown or rebel in most cases.

Adults also have a tendency to forget that they were once a teenager and struggled with some of the same issues: drugs, sex, peer pressure, etc- as the youth do today. If adults would take a quick look back in time and develop a youthful perspective they will find that when they were young they exhibited some of the same bad attitudes, rebellious traits, promiscuity, and other undesirable attributes as some of today's youth. The primary thing young people want adults to do is to be honest about how they were during that period in their life, and stop acting as if they are "Perfect and a Know it all." Adults sharing their struggles with drugs, sex, or any other bad behavior will go a long way in helping give a young person a different perception of a parent or an adult and will start to make them feel that maybe that parent or adult just might able to relate to their current struggles.

Once a connection with that young person has been established it is vital that they communication with them from this point forward using the three R's of communication:

- **Keep it "REAL"**-Talk to them in plain language and be very honest and upfront about your past mistakes. Doing this will help foster a positive relationship with that youngster.

- **Give it to them "RAW"-** Be straight with them. Don't try to dazzle them with "Big" words or treat them like a "Baby" when you are talking. They have heard most terms in the streets, school, home, etc...so give it to them where there can be no misunderstanding, which is the way they are accustomed to communicating.

- **Make it "RELEVANT"-** You must be aware of what's going on with them "NOW" and forget talking about issues in your day because they aren't hearing you - unless you are being honest.

The primary benefit of the three "R"s of communication is that it helps to bridge the disconnection between youths and adults. The task is not difficult. When you think about it we communicate both verbally and nonverbally on a daily basis. The problem today is that we approach the task as a chore. Remember these are the same kids we looked upon with adoration years ago. The only difference today is that most of us have lost our patience and willingness to learn what drives them and the new "slang." Whether we deal with these issues today or tomorrow they will not go away. Time only further expands the gap and makes the transition more difficult.

Time, measured in hours, minutes or days will continue to move. So I ask you, "What happened to the days of yesterday that we refer to as the good ole days?"

TIME MACHINE

It has been said that time brings about a change in everyone. Whether it's a change in weight, hairline, outlook on life, or just a change of address, time has an effect on each of us. So it is very important that today's adults understand that time also has an effect on our current perspective about today's youth. Numerous adults see kids as having "Bad" attitudes, thinking that they know it all, Poor groomers, Sex crazed, etc. However, if each adult would take an honest look back in time to when they were a teenager, and ask themselves the following questions you would find that kids today are not that much different for "us" at the same age. So the challenge is to think back to when you were a teenager and ask yourself the following questions:

1) When I was a teenager what attitude(s) did I exhibit? Many of our attitudes were rebellious and judgmental. Some of the things you would hear from kids back in the day were-"You can't tell me nothing"; "I won't be nothing like my parents when I grow up"; "I know I will be successful." etc.......

2) How your attitude was similar to today's youth? If we are honest most of us would say there are no real differences.

Once you have answered those two questions honestly, we then compare and contrast our youthful attitude perspective to today's youth. How young people deal with authority, group association, and equality issues will have a huge impact on how they live later in life. Going back in time and taking an honest look at our attitudes will help us to start to realize that if we operate from our youthful perspective when dealing with kids, we can begin to further close this disconnection gap.

Now that we are in the proper mind set to make a real effort to work with youngsters it is vital that we begin to understand the three primary forces that drives them.

DRIVING FORCES

There are three primary forces that drive young people today.

They are:

a) The Music they listen to
b) The Media they watch/read (TV, Movies, Books, Video Games, Magazines, etc.)
c) The Peers they associate with in school/community.

History has taught us that you can tell a lot about a person based on what music they listen to, books they read, movies they watch and friends they associate with. So with this thought in mind listening to a youngster genre of music is a big step on the road to understanding them. Keep in mind that all music contains some type of message rather we like what's being said or not. I don't care if that music is Gangster Rap, Rhythm & Blues, Hip-Hop, Heavy Metal, Hard Rock or just good old Gospel music. Most adults have a problem with some of today's music primarily due to the profanity, especially Rap music. Adults have a tendency to tune out or demand that the youngster listen to something else because the profanity either embarrasses or causes discomfort to them. What they fail to realize it the artist is banking on that reaction so that they can deliver the message that is some time hidden beyond the profanity. Adults need to understand that the profanity in most music, in particular rap music, is used to emphasize a point, add shock value, convey a message from the streets, to come across as hard core, or just talk in slang which is full of profanity. Adults need to stop reacting to profanity like they have never heard "cursing" before. Believe it or not these kids are only mimicking us and what they think being an adult is—Cursing, Fussing, Working, Sexing, Drinking, Smoking, etc.

Regardless of the genre of the music that we listen to you will find that it is designed to educate, elevate, negate, mediate, and or regulate. Both todays and yesterday's music tend to deal with many of the same issues and concerns that appear to be circular in nature. At this point we will conduct a lyric comparison and contrast using popular songs and artists in four areas from yesterday and today as it relates to: **Social Issues, Religion, Sex, and Drugs**

MUSIC

When we look at music from back in the day it spoke of social issues and what was going on in America [in particular black America in my opinion] no artists or songs spoke it better then Marvin Gaye and Stevie Wonder. When you look at the lyrics from "What's Going On" you can't help but travel back in time to a place where he talked about war, protest, family struggles, and hate but in the end **Love** was the key to overcoming it all.

Mother, mother There's too many of you crying
Brother, brother, brother
There's far too many of you dying
You know we've got to find a way
To bring some lovin' here today

Father, father
We don't need to escalate
You see, war is not the answer
For only love can conquer hate
You know we've got to find a way
To bring some lovin' here today
Father, father, everybody thinks we're wrong
Oh, but who are they to judge us
Simply because our hair is long
Oh, you know we've got to find a way

To bring some understanding here today

    We followed that piece with Stevie Wonder's "Living for the City" which spoke of Poverty, Family Struggles, etc. In this song, through it all his family gave **Love** and **Affection** to keep him strong and moving in the right direction.

A boy is born in hard time Mississippi
Surrounded by four walls that ain't so pretty
His parents give him love and affection
To keep him strong moving in the right direction

His father works some days for fourteen hours
And you can bet he barely makes a dollar
His mother goes to scrub the floors for many
And you best believe she hardly gets a penny

Both of these songs emphasized the importance of **Love**. From there we move to today's music and two of the most known and popular rappers as it relates to social issues are Tupac and Kanye West.

In Kanye's song entitled, "All Fall Down" he talks about a young lady's struggle as she attempts to be a college student. She majors in a field that *if* she were to graduate, it would pay her low wages. The only reason she has chosen to attend college in the first place is to please her parents though her heart is not committed to it. This song goes on to also talk about struggling with peer pressure as it relates to materials and her real aspiration is to be a hairstylist. Finally it concludes with her having to make a choice between remaining in college or pursuing her real passion of being a hairstylist which in her mind will afford her the opportunity to acquire clothes, car, house, and other things at a faster pace.

Man I promise, she's so self conscious
She has no idea what she's doing in college That major that she majored in don't make no money
But she won't drop out, her parents will look at her funny
Now, tell me that ain't insecure
The concept of school seems so secure
Sophomore three years ain't picked a career She like forget it, I'll just stay down here and do hair
Cause that's enough money to buy her a few pairs of new Airs
Cause her baby daddy don't really care She's so precious with the peer pressure
Couldn't afford a car so she named her daughter Alexus (a Lexus)
She had hair so long that it looked like weave Then she cut it all off now she look like Eve
And she be dealing with some issues that you can't believe
Single black female addicted to retail

In Tupac's, song entitled, "Keep your head up" he talks about encouraging a young single mother who is currently receiving welfare to continue to pursue a better life for herself and her son in spite of the obstacles presented by her present circumstances. He tells her to love herself even when people, especially men, try to put her down. The key to the song is for young women to remain strong and keep their head up. This song also emphasizes that men need to stand up and take care of their responsibilities and help rear their children.

Little something for my godson Elijah and a little girl named Corinne
Some say the blacker the berry, the sweeter the juice
I say the darker the flesh then the deeper the roots
I give a holler to my sisters on welfare
Tupac cares, if don't nobody else care
And I know they like to beat you down a lot
When you come around the block brothers clown a lot
But please don't cry, dry your eyes, never let up
Forgive but don't forget, girl keep your head up
And when he tells you you ain't nothing don't believe him
And if he can't learn to love you you should leave him
Cause sister you don't need him And I ain't tryin to hook up, I just call them how I see them
You know it makes me unhappy When brother make babies, and leave a young mother to be unhappy And since we all came from a woman Got our name from a woman and our game from a woman I wonder why we take from our women Why we rape our women, do we hate our women? I think it's time to kill for our women Time to heal our women, be real to our women
And if we don't we'll have a race of babies That will hate the ladies, that make the babies
And since a man can't make one, He has no right to tell a woman when and where to create one. So will the real men get up I know you're fed up ladies, but keep your head up

When we move to the area of religion, one of the things that stood out from the past was many songs made inferences to issues. Example: God was never said directly, but he was implied. This is evident in the popular song by The Staple singers titled, "I'll Take You There." When you listen to the lyrics, God or Heaven is never mentioned. Yet, we knew exactly what the message in the song referred to.

I know a place, ya'all, Ain't nobody cryin', Ain't nobody worried,
No smilin' faces
(I'll take you there) Mercy now!
I'm callin' callin' callin' mercy(I'll take you there)
Mercy mercy! Let me, I'll take you there
Wanna take you there!
(I'll take you there)
Just take me by the hand Let me
Let me, let me, let me lead the way
Let me take you there
You oughta, you gotta gotta come let me, let me
(I'll take you there)
Take you, take you, take you over there
(I'll take you there)

Critical thinking in the 60's and 70's was emphasized in many educational and home environments. Therefore inference in music was used constantly. To contrast that with today, the song written and recorded by Tupac entitled, "Only God Can Judge Me" both God and Heaven are mentioned directly but the emphasis of the song has no religious message. He talks primarily about betrayal, black on black crime, death, and a few other things.

Only God can judge me, is that right?
Only God can judge me now

Only God baby, nobody else, nobody else All you other folks get out my business
Perhaps I was blind to the facts, stabbed in the back, I couldn't trust my own homies just a bunch a dirty rats
Will I, succeed, paranoid from the weed, And hocus pocus try to focus but I can't see

And in my mind I'm a blind man doing time, Look to my future cause my past, is all behind me, Is it a crime, to fight, for what is mine?
Everybody's dying tell me what's the use of trying, I've been Trapped since birth, cautious, cause I'm cursed, And fantasies of my family, in a hearse

And they say it's the white man I should fear
But, it's my own kind doing all the killing here
I can't lie, ain't no love for the other side
Jealousy inside, make me wish I died
Oh my Lord, tell me what I'm living for
Everybody's dropping got me knocking on heaven's door
And all my memories, of seeing brothers bleed
And everybody grieves, but still nobody sees
Recollect your thoughts don't get caught up the mix, Cause the media is full of dirty tricks

Throughout this song Tupac continues to make the proverbial statement that "Only God Can Judge Me." What happens with most adult when this question is initially raised is their individual view tends to agree or disagree with him when he says, "Only God Can Judge Me."

As we move to the comparison of sexual lyrics, you will find that the clash in value systems really take shape.

Delayed gratification (Lay away mentality) versus Instant gratification (Microwave mentality) is seen exponentially. There were many sexually oriented songs we could select from the 60s and 70s. Two artists who exemplified the boldness in sexual lyrics were Teddy Pendergrass and The O'Jays. Who can refute Teddy Pendergrass' song "Turn off the Lights?" Throughout this song instructions were given, but nothing was said that could be classified as 100% sexual in nature. No doubt we all knew the mood, moment and possible outcome of the encounter.

Let's take a shower, shower together, yeah
I'll wash your body and you'll wash mine, yeah
Rub me down in some hot oils, baby, yeah
And I'll do the same thing to you

Just turn off the lights, come to me
Girl, I wanna give you a special treat, you're so sweet
Turn off the lights and let's get cozy
See, you're the only one in the world that I need

Turn 'em off and come to me
Tonight, I'm in a sexy mood, baby
And light a candle
Girl, there's something that I-I wanna do to you, I wanna do, I wanna do to you, baby
Tell me what you wanna do (There's somethin' I)
Tell me what you wanna do, babe
(There's somethin' I, somethin' I wanna do to you, baby)
Tell me what you wanna do (Yeah)
Tell me what you wanna do, babe (Yes)

Tell me what you wanna do (I've got somethin' in my mind)
Tell me what you wanna do, babe
(Somethin' that I've been wantin' to do all the time, yeah, yes

Tell me what you wanna do (I wanna give you a special treat)
Tell me what you wanna do, babe ('Cause you've been so sweet, yeah, yes)

(Anything that you want, anything that you need, I got it, I got it)

As for The O'Jays many of us assumed that the song, "Stairway to Heaven" referenced religion. A close examination of the lyrics does not support that. Example, "…Here we go…taking the load of this old world off our shoulders. The door is wide open for you the door is wide open for me… still in a moment of pleasure we're gonna find the pirates treasure." Contrary to popular opinion this music was played on gospel radio as religious, yet it was sexual in nature.

Here we go
Climbing the stairway to heaven
Here we go
Walking the road of ecstasy
Taking the load
Of this whole world off our shoulders
The door is wide open for you
The door is open for me

Here we go, Still in a moment of pleasure
You and I
We are gonna find the pirates treasure
Here we go
Climbing the stairway to heaven

And we are going step by step
Together, Step by step
climbing the stairway to heaven
Climbing the stairway to heaven
And we are going step by step
Together Step by step

Put your hand, Lean closer
Don't you wanna go
In our own little corner of the world

When we review sexually explicit lyrics today there is no inference. The message is clear and bold. Youth today do not speak in inference. Songs like Little Wayne's "Lollipop" is the norm not the exception. Example, "But Man I ain't never seen an ass like hers. That pussy in my mouth had me loss for words…She licked me like a lollipop". At this point, How many of you don't know what he is talking about….there is no misunderstanding these lyrics!

Shawty wanna thug
Bottles in the club
Shawty wanna hump
You know I like to touch
Ya lovely lady lumps

Come On Yeah Okay
Lil mama had a swag like mine
She even wear her hair
Down her back like mine

I make her feel right
When its wrong like lyin'
Man she ain't never
Had a love like mine
But Man I ain't never
Seen an ass like hers
That pussy in my mouth
Had me loss for words
Told her to back it up
Like berp berp
And I made that ass jump
Like jerp jerp
And thats when she
She lick me
Like a lollipop (Oh yeah I like that)

When we review Drugs three of more popular artists of the 60s and 70s were The Temptations, Rick James and Curtis Mayfield. Each of these artists had a popular song that referenced drug usage. The Temptations sang of Cloud Nine. This song spoke of LSD and raved, "I'm doing fine up here on cloud nine."

The childhood part of my life wasn't very pretty.
You see, I was born and raised in the slums of the city.
It was a one room shack we slept in, other children beside me.
We hardly had enough food or room to sleep. It was a hard times,
needed something to ease my troubled mind.

My father didn't know the meaning of work. He disrespected Mama
and treated us like dirt. I left home seekin' a job that I never did
find.
Depressed and down-hearted, I took to Cloud 9.
I'm doing...(fine)
Up here. (On cloud nine)
Listen one more time.
I'm doing...(fine)

Up here. (On cloud nine)

Rick James swooned of his lover affair with Mary Jane a.k.a marijuana. He was in love with her and she was his main thing.

I'm in love with Mary Jane.
She's my main thing.
She makes me feel alright.
She makes my heart sing.

And when I'm feeling low,
She comes as no surprise.
Turns me on with her love.
Takes me to paradise.

Do you love me Mary Jane?
Yeah. Whoa-oh-oh.
Do ya? Do ya? Do ya?
Now do you think you love me Mary Jane.

Don't you play no games.
I love her just the same.
I love her, Mary baby, just the same.
The woman plays no games

Curtis Mayfield's song Pusher Man spoke of drug addiction as he rhymed, "I'm your momma, I'm your daddy, I'm that nigga in the alley. I'm you doctor when in need, want some coke? Have some weed…I'm your pusher man."

I'm your Mama I'm your Daddy
I'm that nigga In the alley
I'm your doctor When in need

Want some coke? Have some weed
You know me I'm your friend
Your main boy Thick and thin

I'm your Pusherman (2x)

Ain't I clean Bad machine
Super cool Super mean
Dealin' good For The Man
Superfly
Here I stand Secret stash
Heavy bread Baddest bitches
In the bed

I'm your pusherman (3x)

Silent life of crime A man of odd circumstance
a Victim of ghetto demands
Feed me money for style
And I'll let you trip for a while
Insecure from the past
How long can a good thing last?
Woo-hoo, no...

Got to be mellow, y'all
Gotta get mellow, now

Today's artist we chose for this comparison is Rick Ross. Again there was no inference in the song, "Blow". Blow emphasized the materials that can be gained from selling cocaine. Example: "I got, mo' cars, mo' clothes, mo' money, then smoke mo' blow".

This outta jean, and the head full of dough (Yeah)
Bottle on tha' rose, pass me some mo'
I got, mo' cars, mo' cars, mo' clothes, mo' clothes
Mo' money, then smoke mo' blow (Bloooowwww)
Mo' money, then smoke mo' blow (Bloooowwww)
Mo' money, then smoke mo' blow

Mo' trips, mo' whips, mo' money, I'm mo' rich
Mo' hatas', mo' clips, mo' jewels, mo' chris
Half a hundred grand, this a rubberband
That's all vest, in my other hand
On the other hand, I'm still pitchin' other Hen'
All soft, balls off, bitch a stunna', man
Mo' trucks, mo' bucks, mo' freaks, mo' butts

Adults need to understand that we can learn a lot about our kids by actively listening to the lyrics of the music that they seem to love. What I have found over my 25+ years of working with various types of young people is that deep down most of them want to be accountable and be able to connect with an adult that respects what they listen to without judging them. Believe it or not a lot of kids today are just like yesterday kids in that they do not listen to all the lyrics in a song. Most time it the beat that has their attention and many do not know all the words to the song.

So adults must keep in mind that the music that young people listen to is only one-third of the triangle that appears to have the greatest influence on most of our kids today. We must pay close attention to what they listen to on their iPods, CD players, laptops, ring tones, etc.

MEDIA

The second part of this three headed force is the excessive media that kids are exposed to in today's society. When you do a quick assessment you can easily see that today's youngsters are bombarded with information from every direction. You will find whether it is from the 1000 cable channels, millions of websites, thousands of magazines or millions of books kids are overwhelmed with information and ill equipped to sort out what is "real" versus "fiction".

The media has a great impact on all who view it whether it is the type of television shows watched such as BET, MTV, Sitcoms or *Reality* shows. These shows have a tendency to make young people think that this is how adults are supposed to act. Movies as well have a tendency to be sexual in nature, violent, glorify drugs and fail to show a realistic view of life. Video games played for hours have an influence on young people. Many instances have allegedly occurred where there is a distortion between reality and fiction. An example of this is the cartoon effect which depicts a decapitation where a fictional head runs next to its detached body which is not reality.

Newspapers, magazine or any books read can shape a youngster's view of the outside world. Current fashion and style tends to mimics television and magazine ads. If we compare style of the 60s and 70s of afros and cornrows to dreadlocks, braids, and hair extension of today we find that both are forms of self expression. The question I pose is, "Are the styles today more obscene than the style of the 60s and 70s? Which is more obscene? An afro or dreadlocks?" It really depends on your perspective. Afros were our way of making a visible expression of "blackness." Halter tops expressed freedom from the bra and dashikis proclaimed comfort in clothing. Our parents did not approve of these hairstyles or fashions. As adults today we see the dreadlocks, hair extensions and braiding as extreme, but this is their expression. Our perspectives have changed because this style is so different than what we feel is appropriate. When we compare Hip huggers, bell bottoms and halter tops that young women wore back in the day, we have a hard time relating it to the current style of "sagging." Most young people do not understand the origin of this fashion craze which originated in prison and denoted that you were looking for a same sex relationship. Even the tattooing and Shorty shorts show that youngsters are not aware of the origins of many fashion trends.

PEERS

Peers have the greatest influence on young people and even some adults. These peers can be from school, the local community, church, work and other areas of social interaction. One of the primary reasons gangs are so successful in their recruitment, is because they provide the key elements that young people and adults seek. The key elements are: Safety, Love, Sense of Belonging, Self Worth, Usefulness and Personal Success all with a common goal that appears achievable. Most young people link success to money, clothing, cars and things of that nature. It is imperative that adults understand that it is the peers that youth associate with which currently have the greatest influence in their life. At this stage of life most kids feel that the average adult cannot relate to what they are experiencing thus they have little or no influence on their decision making process. If you review Jawanza Kunjufu's book, The Conspiracy to Destroy Black Boys Volume III, you will find that he talks about the various messages. He does a comparison between the contrasting messages young people receive from both the media and their peers versus the message that they receive from adults.

Microwave Generation vs. Lay-A-Way Generation

MEDIA/PEERS	ADULTS
INSTANT GRATIFICATION	LONG-TERM GRATIFICATION
THEY LISTEN TO EACH OTHER	THEY TALK AT EACH OTHER
SPEND UP TO 8 HRS DAILY	SPEND UP TO 40 MINUTES DAILY
(INCREASES WITH AGE)	(DECREASES WITH AGE)
MATERIALISTIC	MORALITY
MONEY VIA HUSTLE	MONEY VIA EDUCATION

In the chart above you will find that when we refer to instant gratification we see credit cards, microwaves, drive thru restaurants, etc. Under long term gratification we see layaway, home cooked meals, etc.

Most of us when we were young people thought that if we received a good education and worked hard on a job or in life that eventually we would gain the things were wished to acquire in life. Example- Nice home, dream cars, great family and have money in the bank. These were the values we learned from our parents, grandparents or extended family network. This is in stark contrast to youth of today who seek instant gratification. The "Get it Now", "Tomorrow is not promised", "Why wait until tomorrow when you can get it all today", which does not advocate waiting on anything. Everything from clothes, money, events, and even sex has to be done immediately without any delay. Unfortunately this get it quick and get it now mentality sometimes leads to the sale of narcotics, gambling, pursuit an unrealistic professional sport career or music industry career as a rapper, or music producer. These dreams pursued with no backup plan generally leads to committing random crimes.

When you look at the mindset of instant gratification vs. delayed gratification you will find that it is very easy to sale the youth of today a bill of goods. Here is an example of a sales pitch:

- If I can show you a way to gain three times your current income
- Drive the car of your dreams
- Live the life of luxury with all it perks

- And obtain it all in 30 days or less without being arrested. How many people would be interested?

What you find is most people would want to hear what I have to say. This is especially true for a young person who doesn't know how to think critically. Most youth generally want an item, and have no means to get it so this sales pitch is very appealing. They want A (the item) and B (means to obtain item). They don't think about C and D (which are the consequences if they obtain the item illegally). That means that when they obtain this item(s) illegally the repercussions that they may receive include incarceration, probation, loss of future opportunities, and even death. What you will find is that most young people do not know right from wrong. Yes, chronologically they should have been taught right from wrong, but this is our assumption as adults but not necessarily the reality of the situation. Many were never taught to think critically and deduce that if I do A and B, the result will be C and D. Many school curriculums today are focused on standardized testing and there is no emphasis on critical thinking or creative thought processes. So if it is not taught at school, home or in the media, where do they learn it?

They don't unless we as adults whom they respect teach it to them. The sad part is that some time their bad choices result in death because they just happen to be in the wrong place at the wrong time.

BIG QUESTION

So the question must be posed as it relates to youth violence: **"Can the trend relating to youth violence be turned?"** When you look at the problem it is not an easy yes or no answer. Even before you attempt to answer that question you have to view the term THUGS first foremost.

From my vantage point I see THUGS as follows:

Tough to reach individual that most of us don't seem to know how to approach. He appears to be unapproachable. Most Thugs appear to be **H**ateful and uncaring to those who view this person's characteristics from a distance. Some thugs are usually **U**nder educated individuals who work hard at trying to mask their deficiencies through intimidation. We could say that in most cases, this is a **G**odless individual who shows no tendency to worship a supreme being. These individuals usually are **S**eriously deficient in some area. Most are illiterate and have a difficult time expressing themselves, limited work skills and limited coping skills.

However, I also believe Thugs to be a young person "**T**rying **H**ard to **U**nderstand **G**rown folks **S**hit" in the midst of confusing messages being relayed about how to be an adult. Many feel that adult behavior only includes cussing, drinking, smoking and having sex. What you see in many cases, youngsters mimicking what they perceive adult behavior to be from their exposure to adult situations and the media. Adults especially parents need to be mindful that it not what you say to a child that will have the greatest impact but what you do. How you live speaks volumes to a young person.

So with these thoughts in mind we need to look at some strategies to address to overwhelming problem of youth violence in our homes, schools, neighborhoods and society at large.

STRATEGIES

In order to look at any types of strategies or possible solutions to this problem, we must first take a holistic approach in trying to develop some answers to address the four areas or domains that affects each of us. Those areas are: Individual, Family, Community and the Society as a whole. In doing this you will find that the primary one that you will have the greatest impact on is the Individual. Family, Community and Society will be addressed at another time.

Individual-History has shown and my 25+ years of experience working in law enforcement, as a community activist and as a parent of four children substantiates, the number one factor in bridging the disconnect is TIME. When you talk about the TIME you spend with a young person it can be reduced to a very simple acronym:

Total Attention- Turn off the cell phone, television, etc and interact one on one.

Intimate interaction- Here the layers are peeled back and both you and the youth can connect.

Mentor and Mold- Your primary goal is to help shape that young man/woman into the person you want them to be even in your absence later in their life.

Edify and Educate- Here we deal with the Do's and Don'ts. We must teach basic manners because this has great value and will open doors that rudeness will lock.

When you think about the concept of time, most adults if they think back will recall fondly the time they spent with their parents. They recall time spent together versus what their parent bought for them. Time spent had the greatest impact. Nothing can take the place of total attention, interacting, grooming and praising that comes from parents.

Growth and development is another strategy that can be used in helping youth develop their self esteem and improve their overall self worth. Once they understand their history whether it is their family or ethnic history they can see their value. We must emphasize scholarship and education. This is the key to a full and productive life. They must understand heritage and how to deal with peer pressure. We assume they should be able to navigate the problems associated with peers. We must remember that everyone wants to be accepted. The need to be accepted is a critical need and it is important. One of the major things we have lost in the transition is teaching the importance of respect for authority. Respect is a two edged sword. Even though they refuse to be disrespected or "dissed" as they call it. They must give respect to gain respect. When they learn that respect is reciprocal they can relate to the concept of Reaping and Sowing as taught Biblically. These principals will go a long way in helping them to gain success.

We must also teach responsibility. We must show them the importance of accepting responsibility for their actions. Responsible behavior whether it is home, family, work commitments etc., will assist with their overall quest for success. This is a vital component of growth and development. Throughout this entire process adults must learn to actively listen. Listening to what a youth has to say verbally and non verbally. You must learn to read feelings and actions. Once a young adult understands that you are connected to them they will open up and share more. Young adults also feel an inability to bond with adults which we would think should have occurred at a very early age in a child's development. Remember there are varied phases of development and bonding at infancy. We are dealing with young adults and this young person is not the same baby nurtured long ago. They have opinions, aspirations, prejudices and they can be judgmental. Renewed bonding will assist in helping that young person develop intellectually and gain coping skills for difficult situations. The earlier their bond is forged the easier it will be to guide the young adult. Observation skills are paramount if you plan to effectively deal with youths. If a young person says they are doing fine, do not take these words at face value. Watch their behavior and body language. Do their non verbal clues align with what they are verbalizing? A big strategy that most adults need to pay close attention to is Emotional Nutrition.

1. *Adults/Parents must be consistent in keeping regular basic rules. They must devise strategies to deal with confrontations, power struggles and decision making. You cannot be inconsistent when you are trying to help*

youngsters comply with rules. If you allow compromise, you lose credibility.

2. *Adults/Parent must be able to Detoxify or break kids negative patterns of behavior when they are displayed. They must be immediately addressed. Allowing kids to develop bad habits of behavior will eventually lead to more serious acts of rebellion.*

3. *Adults/Parents must be able to draw from a variety of resources and must be able to recognize when they have reached they limits and need outside assistance. This step is difficult for a lot of ethnic groups because the distrust as it relates to allowing outsides to know their private "Business".*

RE-CREATION STRATEGY

There are numerous proven strategies that we can discuss here but the final approach I would like to suggest is a very old one but has stood the test of time and when implemented correctly is very effective in reducing youth violence. This concept is the old Recreation Center Strategy. Now you might say what can the recreation center do? Or you may say we still have these centers and crime has continued to increase. However, if you take a look at how these centers were utilized in the past, as extensions of the family unit, you will find that element is currently missing from most of today's centers. In the past early recreation professionals saw the power of positive discretionary leisure time activities in the development of youth. R*e-creation* is based on the delivery of sports, education and cultural experiences to youth at a multiplicity of risk levels. The re-creation strategy suggests that we must have systems in place to identify risk factors and problem behaviors before we can truly begin to address needs, and build resiliency and competencies in youth. This strategy also builds on the modern day social work practice called "backdoor therapy," which employs the concept of meeting youth where they are.

The chart below talks about the developmental steps based on the fundamental principles of a good Re-Creation strategy

Principles	Trust	Respect	Integrity	Consistency	Self Esteem
Building Competencies	Social	Personal	Citizenship	Belonging	Knowledge, Reasoning and Creativity
Sphere of Influence	Peer	Individual	Community	Family	School
Positive Activities	Sports	Culture	Sports Culture	Culture	Education
Outcomes	Healthy Beliefs and Clear Standards	Opportunities Individual Characteristics	Recognition	Bonding	Skills

(A Youth Development Strategy: Principles to Practice in Re-creation for the 21st Century)

There are many strategies we can suggest that will help in addressing this disconnection between adults and youth of today. Regardless of the strategy you choose to implement our primary job is to be a **Leader** to our youth and that means:

Love Them
Encourage Them
Assist Them
Direct Their Path
Educate Them
Respect Their Person

When we as adults can start to do these things we begin slowly X out the media box by standing in the gap as a viable alternative source of knowledge for our youth. By developing a viable and sound plan for connecting with our young people and implementing it correctly, we remove ourselves from that state of dreading what the future holds instead we embrace the future with great expectations.

CLOSING

The issues facing teens today are much greater than those facing youth in the past. There needs to be a comprehensive risk reduction and youth development strategy implemented to meet youth where they are in communities. By working to reduce harmful risks, meet physical, mental and emotional needs, and build competencies, we can truly reclaim, rebuild and restore essential bonds between youth and community development. Re-creation programming can serve to provide opportunities for individuals, families and communities to come together to work on issues that adversely affect their environments. For many years adults have pre-determined what the best strategies are to address youth needs without hearing from youth themselves. As a youth advocate, I believed I knew what was best for youth. After listening to youth in a variety of settings, I was quickly reminded that I have no youth voice and cannot adequately represent all of what works for youth unless I ask them and bring their voices forward to represent their own views. When we take the time to solicit a youthful perspective, we will gain a deeper sense of what the young people of today have to deal with as it relates to their homes, school, community and the various personal relationships they have developed at this point in their lives.

When we as adults come to realize and accept that the youth of today are technologically smarter, more confrontational, self centered and less forgiving then the youth of yester years, the task of connecting with and guiding of our future leaders is less overwhelming and very manageable.

About The Author

Randolph Bernard Lewis was born in Jacksonville, Florida on May 4, 1959. Mr. Lewis is the sixth child in a family of nine children reared in a two parent household in an economically depressed neighborhood on the northwest quadrant of the city. During his formative years, Mr. Lewis, in addition to his siblings and parents he lived in a three bedroom home with an additional eleven extended family members. The realization that they were poor wasn't revealed to him until 1974 upon entering high school at Jean Ribault Senior High. Upon entering high school as a 10th grade student he quickly discovered that most of the students in his school did not share clothing with their siblings nor did they receive Christmas gifts issued through community outreach programs. Prior to 1974 he knew that it was the love and encouragement given to him at home and at his church that kept him sheltered from the realities of poverty. He stated that he did not know that their annual summer camp excursions with his church were underwritten by generous donations from members in our congregation. He goes on to say that some of his greatest memories were he and his peers spending all of their free time at the community church playing sports and participating in youth programs. The church involvement experienced by himself and his siblings was the result of a very generous pastor, Reverend Rudolph W. McKissick, Sr., who was deeply troubled that children living in the community were not a part of the sanctuary and benefiting from the programs established. The children of the Lewis household were invited into an elite upscale religious edifice on the condition that they attend services if they wanted to participate in the church's many activities. It was during that period of Mr. Lewis' life that he was transformed by the teachings, encouragement and generosity of the pastor and his congregation. The children were taught that education was the key to success and athletics could underwrite the cost.

Prior to sixth grade Mr. Lewis attended a nonintegrated educational institution. When the city of Jacksonville integrated its public schools, he experienced a number of personal changes. Along with puberty, he experienced the ills associated with early integration. When Mr. Lewis arrived at school, he and the other students were greeted with racial slurs and tension that many communities experienced during those early days of change. Mr. Lewis, states that he realized at an early age that the "haters" reaction was fear of the unknown. He too was fearful and yet somewhere deep inside he held on to the seed planted earlier that the education he received would be the key to something better even though he did not know what that something was. Mr. Lewis excelled academically and integrated the school's baseball team. The young men "trying out" for the team were cautioned not to get their hopes up, yet Mr. Lewis shares that he attended "try outs" knowing," If they see me play, they'll pick me for the team" and he was right. Year later Mr. Lewis would look back at that experience and realize that once our integrated baseball team adopted the same mission (to win) the color barrier neutralized - on the field and they became many athletes but one team.

In 1977, Mr. Lewis became the oldest child at home following his parent's separation. By this period of his life his extended family had moved out of his parents home years earlier and his older siblings/cousins were attending various colleges earning Bachelor's and Master's degrees. Following high school he became the primary provider of the home and delayed his dream to go to college and play baseball. His mother could not work due to serious health ailments. During those years of work, Mr. Lewis attended community college and maintained a decent grade point average. A few years passed and following his brother's return home from the army, he proceeded to market himself to several schools and ultimately gained an athletic scholarship to Bethune -Cookman College to underwrite his college expenses. Mr. Lewis attended college as an older student. He arrived on campus determined to excel academically and grateful for the opportunity. His colleagues and team mates perceived him as "happy go lucky", but they were not aware of the struggles he had endured prior to becoming an undergraduate student. Many years have passed since those early days of poverty. He has completed his bachelors and masters degree. He has have help establish outreach programs and has mentored young males within the community for over twenty five years conveying the importance of education. He has touched the lives of "budding athletes" as an athletic coach and many of those young men became athletic standouts in high school, intercollegiate and professional sports. By stature he is a big guy, however by nature he is a mild tempered and calm spirit. He enjoys making friends and claims to have never met a person who did not become his friend on some level.

Throughout his personal and professional career Mr. Lewis has worked with diverse communities including: Asians, Hispanic, Cubans, Russians, Europeans and Haitians to name a few. Rather personally or professionally he has found that we all seem to want the same things in life and that is to receive Respect, Understanding, and the Opportunity to make a good living. This is called community empowerment: Community's sense of self-control, Dignity, and Self-respect.

These and other experiences have led him in making a commitment to development of workshops that improve services to diverse groups. Mr. Lewis has found that the essence of empowerment is gaining a sense of personal and group control. Community empowerment is achieved through its citizens engaging in activities that improve the quality of life and respond to community needs.

Mr. Lewis is the President of Lewis Maxwell Training Consultants, Inc., a multidimensional Education, Business and Criminal Justice Training firm based in St. Petersburg, Florida. He is also employed as a Criminal Justice Project Coordinator II with Southeastern Public Safety Institute at St. Petersburg College where he facilitates In-service Criminal Justice training for both Law Enforcement and Corrections Personnel. Mr. Lewis holds a Bachelor of Science degree in Business Administration and a Master's of Arts degree in Criminology. Mr. Lewis has served as an adjunct professor on the staff of the University of South Florida, Florida Metropolitan University and St. Petersburg College. He has served as a consultant with 21st Century Research & Evaluations and Criminal Justice Training & Education Companies based in Tallahassee, Florida as well as the Pinellas County Police Athletic League. He has served as a program moderator/presenter at the 9th, 20th 23rd 24th and 25th Annual National Conference on Preventing Crime in the Black Community and holds memberships within various professional and civic organizations. Mr. Lewis' wealth of knowledge, diverse background and energetic instructional program incorporates lecture, role-playing and application of materials into an outstanding educational environment.

Family

Lewis Family Photo 1970s

Britteny Lewis' Graduation from BCU

The Lewis Family 2010

The Good Ole' Days

Randy Lewis 6th Grade

Student Athlete 1982

Bethune Cookman College (BCC) Student 1982

Mentors & Mentoring

Bishop McKissick, Sr., GV & Lafayette

GV, Bishop McKissick, Sr & Me

Pathfinder's Sickle Cell Project

Omegas & DelTeens

Young Gentlemen of Distinction (YGOD)

Uplift & Brotherhood

NABCJ Training Ohio

Office of Attorney General Conference

"Bruhs" at Pathfinder Function

Breakfast with Santa

Feed the Children Event

Relay for Life

References

Bembry, Reco. A Youth Development Strategy: Principles to Practice in Re-creation for the 21st Century: *Journal of Park and Recreation Administration*, 1998, 17(2), 15-34.

Birdsong, R. and N.A.D. Jackson (2000). Coaching Your Kids in the Game of Life. Minneapolis: Bethany House Publishers.

Religion and Ethics: Mentoring Inner City Boys. http://www.pbs.org/wnet/religionandethics/week1008/feature.html

Kunjufu, Jawanza: Countering the Conspiracy to Destroy Black Boys

Kunjufu, Jawanza: Black Economics: Solutions for Economic and Community Empowerment

Leary, Joy Degruy Ph.D.(2005). Post Traumatic Slave Syndrome. Oregon:Upton Press

www.ingramcontent.com/pod-product-compliance
Lightning Source LLC
Chambersburg PA
CBHW031214090426
42736CB00009B/914